This book is dedicated to my parents. For my mom, C'panions, and in the memory of my late dad, Joseph; both of whom have influenced my love for entrepreneurship and my reverence for God. They both were business leaders at one point or another before retirement.

D1500892

Acknowledgments

First and foremost, I thank my terrific parents: my mom, C'panions Andrews, for her many blessings and for believing in me and my abilities. Mom has been a rock and a great support. Thank you, mom. My late father, Joseph Antoine, was a phenomenal example of a great entrepreneur and his love still lives on in my heart.

I'm also incredibly fortunate to have such a fantastic support system from family and friends. My aunties, uncles, mentors, and colleagues have all played a crucial role in my journey. Without their support, I wouldn't be where I am today.

I'm grateful for my significant other, E'jaaz A. Siddiqui. He's been one of my biggest cheerleaders, always encouraging me to dig deep and never give up. Thank you, Sid! And of course, I am incredibly thankful for my siblings. My sister, Nekesha Andrews-Duprey, has been my confidante and sounding board, always there to listen and offer her unconditional love. My brother, Lyndon Sorzano, has been in my corner as a rock and one of my main supporters, encouraging me when needed.

I thank my aunties Loanne Andrews, Calistra Isaura Andrews, Agatha Lauren Andrews, Thelva Andrews-Guy, Cindy Andrews, Andrea Andrews, and my uncles Alston Andrews, and Reginald Andrews, for being who they are and for their faith in me. Thank you, family.

I thank my amazing mentors Willa Hall Smith and Maudine R. Cooper; they have always been there for me no matter what. I am uncertain how people make it in life without these kinds of people. They have always been kind, loving, and ready to give me a wise word whenever needed. Thank you, amazing women.

I am grateful for some of the people whose support I have had over the years; Blessing Adore, Michael Bernard, Heather Bernier, Brenda Billingy, Arlene Brown, Carl Clarke, Bernadette Clay, Verna Coombs, Chris King-David, Sandra Dawson, Bernard Duprey, Cora Edwards, Maudette Edwards, Evan George, Taylor Groupe, Edwin Guandique, Afer Jackson, Isata Jalloh, Colin Jeffers, Trevor Kinlock, Ella Kumi, Decarla Martin, Daniel McDonald,,Earl McLaren, Charles W. McNiell Jr, Helianthe Monkou, Neil J. Moore, Andrea Pelham, Bernadine Pierre-Andrews, Terry Ann Pollidore Sorzano, Janice Powell, Guiselly Astrid Erazo Romero, Calvin Smith, Janice E. Smith, Yas Soroush-Haq, Dennis C. Sorzano, Dennis J. Sorzano, Gavrielle L. Sween, Betty Taylor, Gillian Thomas, and so many others. I also extend my gratitude to the Business Success Group.

And last but certainly not least, I want to thank God almighty. He's been the constant in my life, giving me the passion and love for others and for desiring success for them. I owe everything to Him.

Foreword

Being an entrepreneur can be quite rewarding. There are the highs when business is thriving and employees are acting right, and you are receiving the exposure that your business needs to prosper. There can also be the lows, the times that you may feel like everything is crumbling, fear envelopes you, and you may feel that you should give up on your entrepreneurial journey. Your journey can be one of success.

This devotional was written with all entrepreneurs in mind. God cares about your success as an entrepreneur and once you cast your plans in His hands, He will take those plans and make it beautiful. You will be totally amazed at the success and overflowing abundance that this act can create. You will receive eagle success.

The eagle is a powerful animal, and it does not settle for mediocrity. It always soars when it takes flight. It is consistently steady. That is the kind of success you can experience as you move through these forty days of earnestly devoting yourself and your business to God.

Forty usually signifies a time of testing, trial, purification, and renewal. The number 40 is significant in this work, because it is the time for a total transformation in the way you operate as a business owner. It allows you to set the pace for consistency, determination, and the ultimate success through assessment, renewal, and recommitment.

This 40-day devotional sets the pace each day for 40 days for you as a business owner to transform your thoughts and realign with the power that God has already placed within your mind. It is designed for a daily rendezvous with God. At the end of the 40 days, you have the potential to be renewed and ready for soaring success, just like the eagle.

Author's Reflections

As businesses play a crucial role in our lives and in the world, it is essential to understand that building a successful enter-prise takes time, effort, and a clear purpose. To help entre-preneurs and business leaders achieve success, I offer a spiritual perspective that emphasizes the power of the mind and the guidance of God.

This book is designed to inspire and encourage readers to tap into the mental power that God has instilled within us and to run their businesses with His guidance. While I understand that money is often a concern for business owners and that people want to see immediate results, this devotional is not intended to deliver quick fixes. Rather, it is crafted to be read over 40 days, with short and easy daily readings that are intentionally designed to be simple and straightforward.

The journey outlined in this book can be repeated as many times as needed and can even be done with an accountability partner to help keep you on track. It is essential to make a commitment to yourself at the end of the 40 days, as a daily review of this commitment can work wonders for you as an entrepreneur.

The truth is that God is interested in every aspect of our lives, including our businesses. The word of God includes many principles applicable to running a successful business. While I am not advocating for business owners to walk around quoting scriptures, I am advocating for us to run our businesses with the understanding that we can be successful if we purposefully allow the omniscient and all-powerful God to help us.

Ephesians 3:20 states, "Now unto Him who is able to do exceedingly abundantly above all that we can ask or think according to the power that works in us..." The message in this text should make us shout for joy and anticipation. Just imagine that God can do more than you can imagine, ask, or think. He can do more than what you desire most for your business. I genuinely hope you will take this message to heart and allow God to take your business beyond what you can imagine.

Day One

"But they that wait upon the LORD shall renew
their strength; they shall mount up with wings
as eagles; they shall run, and not be weary; and
they shall walk, and not faint." Isaiah 40:31

When I think of the eagle, I think of soaring. God
wants us to wait on him and he will make us soar
like the eagle. We will work in our business and on our business, yet we will not be tired. We will be strong and resilient.
This is the promise that God gave us in His Word.

Often, entrepreneurs may think of quitting, but God
asks us to wait because he will give us renewal of strength.
He will not only renew our physical strength, but he will in
fact renew our mental, spiritual and financial strength.
When God does something, He does it well. He goes all the
way and when He renews our strength, we will indeed be
strong. We will be strong throughout every area of our life
including our business.

Waiting is not the act of doing nothing. It is the act of
being aware, to anticipate and to listen. In the period of
waiting, we should not waste time, because waiting is active
not passive. We can trust God and wait for Him to renew
our business and anticipate hearing from Him regarding our
next business move.

The important thing is to wait for God and allow Him
to renew us. Running ahead of God is not the answer. He is

all-knowing and because He is, and we are not, then it is safe to trust Him completely with our business. Accept that the renewal He is offering us is indeed paramount. When someone gives us a gift, we usually accept it. God is giving us the gift of renewal. Accept His gift and prepare to receive it daily and especially in the quiet of the early morning, God will provide the renewal that we need. He knows just what we need to prosper in our business. He knows the clients we need. He can and will guide our clients to us because he knows that we have what they need. Let us trust God totally with our life as an entrepreneur and He will cause us to soar.

~

Quiet Reflections

_____

_____

_____

_____

_____

_____

_____

_____

_____

_____

Day Two

"And he called his ten servants, and delivered them ten pounds, and said unto them, Occupy till I come." Luke 19:13

There is a saying I have that reminds me of the message of this text. It is "don't just live and die, do something meaningful in between." The essence of this saying is to "occupy till Christ comes." There may be times that you feel the need to do nothing. It is important to rest and do nothing at times. However, taking daily actions to bring us closer to our business goals will help us to achieve them.

After all, the Bible says to occupy until Christ comes. Occupy can mean to be busy in our business, busy being faithful - faithful to ourselves, to God, to others and to our business. There is no point in running a business without being faithful to it. Do what is necessary to run the business successfully. Away with the excuses. Yes, I said it, excuses. Though it may not be what you want to hear, it is said in love for us and what we have set out to accomplish. We must move forward faithfully daily planning our work and working our plan as we build upon each day to successfully run our business.

Intentionally thinking of how we would like to occupy this earth as a person and as a business owner can make a world of a difference for us in our business. Let us be intentional in our business dealings and the daily operations of our business. In the end, we will reap the rewards of success.

~

Quiet Reflections

_____

_____

_____

_____

_____

_____

_____

_____

_____

_____

Day Three

"Thou shalt not defraud thy neighbor, neither rob him: the wages of him that is hired shall not abide with thee all night until the morning." Leviticus 19:13

As an entrepreneur, we most times have employees or contractors. Basically, there are people whom we must pay, because they work for us in some capacity. Being eagle-minded is paying these workers as they should be paid. It is not holding back from them, given that they have worked diligently for us.

We are encouraged to not only pay the workers but also pay them timely. This is sometimes tough for an entrepreneur to balance the books and make payments to workers. It is important to trust God and follow His word as He commands us as business owners to refrain from withholding pay that is due to workers.

Reviewing the payroll and ensuring that our workers are being paid fairly and timely is an act of being eagle minded. Additionally, these workers will continue to provide us with great service because they are being paid well. God's vision for us is not for us to display a spirit of lack and not enough in our business. He desires that we move forward successfully and profitably.

Following God's command to pay our workers (contractors included) is not only for those we hire. It is also for those who provide a service to us and did not charge us. Offer those people a payment for their time, skills, and resources. Let them tell us that it is a gift. Remember that people have bills just like we do, and their time and service should never be taken for granted. It is very nice to receive free stuff but is very rewarding to compensate others. We should be ready and willing to pay our workers and those who provide value for and to us. It is the right thing to do as a business owner.

∾

Quiet Reflections

_____

_____

_____

_____

_____

_____

_____

_____

_____

_____

Day Four

"Bring ye all the tithes into the storehouse, that there may be meat in mine house, and prove me now herewith, saith the Lord of hosts, if I will not open you the windows of heaven, and pour you out a blessing, that there shall not be room enough to receive it." Malachi 3:10

The word of God is clear that tithing is powerful. Just imagine God opening the windows of heaven and pouring us out overflowing blessings that we do not have enough room to receive it. Let us hold that vision in our mind's eye.

Giving back to God provides for overflow. There are many ways that you, as an entrepreneur, can give back to God. The bible calls for a tenth of our earnings. This is the most precise way to return to God. Additional ways to give back to God are by donating to the poor and needy, or to organizations that serve the less fortunate, purchasing food or clothing to give to the shelters, orphanages, unofficially adopting a child who is less fortunate by sending them funds or meeting their needs notwithstanding the part of the world that they are located.

There are many entrepreneurs who have remained consistent with giving back to God and their blessings remain consistent. It is not that if we don't give back, God will withhold blessings from us; it simply means that if we as entrepreneurs are obedient to this command, we will be wowed by how our business flourishes.

It is indeed a tough call for some given that all entrepreneurs have expenses that must be met monthly. As a matter of fact, some entrepreneurs cannot afford to meet their expenses monthly. I get it, on top of that asking for a business owner who is not financially stable to give up ten percent of their earnings may sound like a tall order. Seeing the blessings that come will outweigh the sacrificial giving if this act of tithing is exercised consistently.

Why not try it today? There will be no regrets. Let us promise ourselves that once we see the benefits of tithing that we will not only continue to tithe faithfully, but also share its benefits with others.

~

Quiet Reflections

_____

_____

_____

_____

_____

_____

_____

_____

_____

_____

Day Five

"Be careful for nothing; but in everything by prayer and supplication with thanksgiving let your requests be made known unto God." Philippians 4:6

L et me meet payroll, let me get 100 new clients within the next 30 days, let me make $1 million dollars this year. These are just some of the requests that entrepreneurs may make, either aloud or silently. There may be other types of requests that we make. We make these requests of God and tend to worry about them at the same time.

We tend to become nervous about some of our requests because we do not fully believe that God can do exactly what we ask for and even more. He can fulfill our every request. As humans, we tend to think of God as limited. This may sound strange to the ear of the Christian entrepreneur. However, if we are doubtful in our requests to God, we are by extension doubtful of God Himself.

When we come to God in prayer and we make our requests, we must firmly believe that He can and will hear our prayers and act on them. We should believe nothing else. In the space of that complete faith is where we see our biggest answers to prayers. Test it out.

When we see our operating expenses measured against our revenue, we may sometimes shudder in our proverbial boots and our minds may start racing to fix the picture. It is good that we want to fix the picture. Not only must we fix the picture, but we must also indeed fix the reality. But how?

The Bible asks us to "be careful for nothing." This means that we need not worry. Instead, we are asked to make our requests known to God through prayer, supplication, and thanksgiving. Whenever we think to ask God for things, let us remember this request that God asks of us.

~

Quiet Reflections

_____

_____

_____

_____

_____

_____

_____

_____

_____

_____

Day Six

"I can do all things through Christ which
strengtheneth me." Philippians 4:13

We can achieve whatever goals we set for ourselves!
Let's be clear about this. If we can imagine it, we
can accomplish it. The Bible tells us that we can do all
things...not some things, not one thing, not part of a thing,
but ALL things.

We should be inspired by the Bible's message. There is
nothing that we cannot do with God's help. The next part
of the verse says, through Christ who strengthens me. God
gives us the power to do all things. If we have set goals, and
we start doubting whether we can reach them, then we are
letting fear and uncertainty destroy our dreams before they
even take shape, before they even start growing. Instead, let
us nourish our dreams with the "I can do" attitude no
matter what.

No matter how bleak things look, no matter how weak
we feel, no matter who tells us that we can't, no matter how
low the budget is, no matter what obstacles are in our way,
just get past all of that and know and believe that you can.

There are many examples of people around us who have
said that they can and they did. On the other hand, there are
many around you who hesitated and they are still struggling

to achieve even one of their goals. If you have been hesitating and you want to change the direction of your life, YOU CAN do it.

The first step is to change your mindset. Start telling yourself that you can. Say it now, "I can do all things." Say it again, "I can do all things." One more time, "I can do all things!" Now that you have affirmed that in this moment, please keep reaffirming that today and always.

God cannot lie, and if He said you can do all things, then trust Him, because you absolutely can!

~

Quiet Reflections

_____

_____

_____

_____

_____

_____

_____

_____

_____

_____

Day Seven

"Beloved, I wish above all things that thou mayest prosper and be in health, even as thy soul prospereth." 3 john 1:2

It has been said that "our health is our wealth." This is true - without our health, we will not be able to enjoy our wealth. As a result, it will be as though we have no wealth.

What is the point of working diligently to achieve our goals for financial success and wealth if we have not been taking care of our health? We might as well stop, because our health is really a priority over seeking wealth. Some business owners rise early and go to bed extremely late. A senior citizen once told me that, *for health and long life, never burn the candles at both ends of the stick.* She stressed how important it was to rest. Some entrepreneurs can attest to the fact that it may be hard to rest when the business and its success depend on them. However, focusing on health and wellness will free up our ability to drive success on a consistent basis.

God said in His word that He wishes above all things that we prosper and be in good health. Bringing health and prosperity together is a very important and intentional undertaking. If God has pronounced His desire for both our health and wealth success, then all we have to do is claim it and walk in it.

What are you doing today to walk in health and prosperity? Be intentional and explode your blessings of health and wealth.

~

Quiet Reflections

_____

_____

_____

_____

_____

_____

_____

_____

_____

_____

Day Eight

"And the Lord shall make thee the head, and not the tail; and thou shalt be above only, and thou shalt not be beneath; if that thou hearken unto the commandments of the Lord thy God, which I command thee this day, to observe and to do them." Deuteronomy 28:13

Having most of the market share in your industry is admirable. Being known for your goods or service is a position that every entrepreneur finds exciting. After all, if you have a large percentage of market share and you are well-known for your goods or services, this means that your business is flourishing. It really means that you are the head within your industry. You are not the tail.

The word of God states that the Lord will make you the head and not the tail. This is very exciting for a business owner to be placed above and never below. Imagine being the top business in your industry. It is possible, because the word of God says so.

There is a way that you can achieve being the head and being above. That is if you listen, follow and do the commands of God. How can you listen and follow the commands of God? The only way to do so is to daily dig into His word, maintain a daily devotion and communicate with God. That relationship with God will develop and flourish more than you can imagine. He will walk and talk with you. He will give you the wisdom you need to run your business successfully. He will make you the head and not the tail. You will be above and not below.

How? Study His words, listen to His commands and do them. This is all that God is asking. He will give you the success that you desire. Sometimes it may seem difficult to stay in tune with God as an entrepreneur given all the intricacies that can come with running a business. The truth is that it is very possible to remain attuned to what God wants you to do. If it were impossible, God would not have asked us to do it.

Go out today and be the head, be above, because that is what God wants for you.

~

Quiet Reflections

_____

_____

_____

_____

_____

_____

_____

_____

_____

_____

Day Nine

"And I have filled him with the spirit of God, in wisdom, and in understanding, and in knowledge, and in all manner of workmanship..." Exodus 31:3

Running a business is not an easy task, especially when you first get started. You keep working on the plan for success and revising it where necessary. You may feel like you need to do that particular thing to achieve breakthrough success. You may feel like you are doing everything that you should and not seeing the success that you see other entrepreneurs experiencing.

If you allow Him, God will fill you with wisdom, understanding and knowledge. He will equip you with the wisdom required to take your business to the next level. He will grant you the understanding necessary to observe the marketplace, taking you and your business to the rightful place to gain a competitive advantage. He will give you the knowledge base to be consistent in delivering exceptional goods and services to your customers and clients. That is the kind of God that we serve.

Yes, God is an amazing entrepreneur. He knows all business types inside out. He is a business guru actually. He is all-knowing and all-wise, even in business – any kind. There is nothing that He does not know or cannot do. He knows exactly each step that you should take to reap resounding success and exponential profit.

As an entrepreneur, give your business back to God. If He chooses, He can take it, because He gave it to you in the first place. Give it back to Him of your free choice. If you have not yet dedicated your business to God, find the time and do it. You can make it as fancy or as simple as you choose, just make sure you are sincere. Just like you give your children back to God through a dedication, or you give your house back to God through a house blessing, do give your business back to Him too. You will be happy that you did.

~

Quiet Reflections

_____
_____
_____
_____
_____
_____
_____
_____
_____
_____

Day Ten

"Commit to the Lord whatever you do, and
he will establish your plans." Proverbs 16:3

E very business should have a strategic plan. Many goals
and action items are derived from the strategic plan. I
suggest to you that God will establish your plans if you
commit to Him whatever you do.

Have you already entrusted your business to God? If
not, it is not too late. Commit your business to God, the
physical building (if you have one) and the daily business
operations, the employees, the clients, vendors and all stakeholders. Once you commit whatever you do to God, He will
set your business apart from the others in your industry.

Having a business plan is one of the steps that distin-
guishes your business. Imagine having someone to review
your plans, telling you exactly the revisions you need to
make and how to activate the plan effectively to maximize
your profits. This does not have to be only in your imagina-
tion. It can be a reality. You see, God can and will take a
strong interest in the success of your business if you commit
it to Him. Committing your business to God is not a one-
time affair, it should be a consistent and daily occurrence.
The way you do this is to review your plans and business
before Him each day, asking Him to establish your plans.

Ask Him to uphold your strategic plans and your daily plans. He will guide you and He will put others in your path to help you with your business success.

The first step is to implement a practice to commit your business plans to God daily. The rest of it will follow and you will be amazed at the magnitude of the success you will experience.

~

Quiet Reflections

_____

_____

_____

_____

_____

_____

_____

_____

_____

_____

Day Eleven

"In all toil there is profit, but mere talk tends only to poverty." Proverbs 14:23

We have probably all heard the saying that "talk is cheap." Literally, it is, especially when no action follows the talk.

If you want to make a profit in your business, you can. Think of all that you can do to make a profit, discuss it with God and with the appropriate persons as applicable. Then, implement tools while taking the necessary actions towards that end. Merely talking about your desire to make a profit is not enough. If you only talk about it, then lack is bound to show up among other undesirable results. Working towards the profit guarantees that you will reap it.

Generate profit by working towards it. Sitting back and talking about it will result in nothing. Talking is very important, because we must "speak those things as though they were..." Talking also helps to lodge it further in your subconscious, which is very important. Being that our mind is very powerful, whatever we put in will certainly show itself at some point in some way. Therefore, talking is critical.

If you are only talking, that is when the issue of struggle and lack of profit arises. Take the time required to examine your business. If you are making a profit, I guarantee that you did not do it by merely talking. You had to work - you had to take some action. On the other hand, if you are unfortunately not making a profit, see if you are doing the work or if you are only talking. If you are talking and working, but you have not seen business profit, keep working. It is said in the Word that there is profit in work. Certainly, this is part of it and a major factor. There are other factors that help to make that profit. Today, know that your work will bring you a profit.

~

Quiet Reflections

_____

_____

_____

_____

_____

_____

_____

_____

_____

_____

Day Twelve

"Whatsoever thy hand findeth to do, do it with thy might; for there is no work, nor device, nor knowledge, nor wisdom, in the grave, whither thou goest." Ecclesiastes 9:10

When you work in your business, do it with determination, diligence and consistency. As somber as it may be, the reality is that in the grave you cannot work, think, develop knowledge, tools, or anything. You may as well do all you can now!

Make a mark in this world. Go hard in your business. This does not mean working hard without leisure time or spending time with family and friends. What it means is to work smarter and not necessarily harder. Working smarter involves doing your best on a consistent basis. It means being an example for your employees, colleagues and those who may be looking at you from a distance without your knowledge. When you wear the hat of diligence, the lives of others will be impacted whether you realize it or not. Your life and your business will also be impacted. All of it in a positive and admirable way.

When you want to improve client or customer experience, assess whether you are being diligent in your business. It may seem as though you are not directly responsible for customer experience. As the head of any business, you are directly responsible for this aspect of your business. Think of yourself as being the brain of your business and all your body parts as your employees. When the brain tells the body part what it should do and how it should function, things work in harmony to achieve the goal at hand. Let's say that the brain tells the hand to write a thank you note. Not only do the hands have to be activated for this task, but also the fingers, the eyes, and muscles. Let's stop there without getting too deep into the physiology of it all. You get the point; as the head, you are responsible. Now that we are on the same page, go out today and every day and whatever you do in and for your business, do it with all your might - practicing determination, diligence and consistency.

~

Quiet Reflections

_____
_____
_____
_____
_____
_____
_____
_____
_____
_____

Day Thirteen

"But remember the Lord your God, for it is
he who gives you the ability to produce
wealth." Deuteronomy 8:18

Business owners are in business to serve and to create wealth. Given this, it would behoove you as a business owner to discover how you can produce the wealth that you desire. The good news is that God desires that you prosper. He is the one who gives you the wisdom that causes you to produce wealth. There is a requirement, however.

The requirement is to remember the Lord your God. Remembering God means that you maintain a relationship with Him just like you would with a friend. Treat Him as you would treat a best friend. Do not shove Him aside until you want something that you know He can give. Keep Him close even if you are not in need at a particular period.

God can do anything and He can give anything. Most of us know that already and we believe it even if on the surface in some cases. Remembering God means to connect with Him on a deep level. It does not mean to cry out to Him only when things go wrong in your business. Having a strong communication with Him to the extent that you tell Him the good as well as the not-so-good is important for success. Like with any relationship, without communication, it will not survive. Therefore, keep the communication alive between you and God.

Tell God what you would like to see in your business. He cares about it, can and will give your business success. He will show you how to proceed in your business dealings. He will give you the right employees, business associates, business partners and resources. He is that kind of a God. One of the requirements is to remember Him.

~

Quiet Reflections

_____

_____

_____

_____

_____

_____

_____

_____

_____

_____

Day Fourteen

"For we are God's handiwork, created in Christ Jesus to do good works, which God prepared in advance for us to do." Ephesians 2:10

We read, watch, or listen to the news on mainstream media or social media almost daily for some of us. Others who refuse to make the news a part of their lives, friends and family, though unsolicited, ensure you know what is going on. Sometimes the news can be daunting. Let's face it, at times we wonder if things can get any worse, just when we think things are under control, the unthinkable surfaces.

Business owners help build the fabric of society and by extension of the world in which we live. We can help shape the world. We are God's handiwork and He created us to do good works. If we are following God, we will not only do good in our part of the globe, but also, we will spread good. If each business owner thinks of ways to spread good and executes on the thought, what beauty can exist in our world.

The good news is that there are some businesses that take doing good very seriously and they make it a part of their culture and daily operations. There are other businesses that would focus on doing good if they did not have to think of meeting payroll or paying expenses. God has prepared us as business leaders in advance. We are to slow down, refocus our proverbial lenses and prioritize.

Giving priority to doing good as a business owner will make God pleased and your business will have a better chance to prosper the way it should. Be creative, innovative and think of ways that your business can give back and help make the world a better place. Show up in this world as giving back and let your business be known as one that does good – embrace social responsibility.

~

Quiet Reflections

_____

_____

_____

_____

_____

_____

_____

_____

_____

Day Fifteen

"For I know the plans I have for you,"
declares the LORD, "plans to prosper you
and not to harm you, plans to give you hope
and a future." Jeremiah 29:11

Sometimes in your entrepreneurial journey, you may feel hopeless. Reviewing your financials, looking at industry forecasts, examining your client numbers, can all have a daunting effect on you depending on where you are in your mindset and business.

God has declared that He knows the plans for you. If someone knows something that you want to know, you will try to find out. Since God already knows the plans He has for you, the logical step to take is to find out from Him about those plans. He is open to sharing those plans with you. God's plans for you include your business. He cares about your business success, because He cares about you and anything related or affiliated with you. He has already established that His plans for you are to prosper and not to harm you.

God plans to prosper you. The human in you may wonder: *how will He prosper me?* He has given you tools that will bring you prosperity. One of those tools is your business. Another of those tools is your mind power.

He wants you to use your mind and activate it to believe firmly in "a hope and a future" that He designed specifically for you and your business. There is no need to ever feel hopeless because the creator of the Universe has a specific plan to prosper you that does not include harm, but that includes hope and a future.

Claim this plan and promise. It is available to you without a cost.

~

Quiet Reflections

_____

_____

_____

_____

_____

_____

_____

_____

_____

_____

Day Sixteen

"You need to persevere so that when you have done the will of God, you will receive what he has promised." Hebrews 10:36

God has numerous promises in His word for entrepreneurs. To receive those promises, He has asked you to persevere and do His will.

Perseverance is essential for success. After the first obstacle, you cannot give up. You must be determined and look for ways to overcome each obstacle. Other business owners may have overcome the very same obstacle that you may face in your business. There is no need to reinvent a way forward. Use the map left by others. The key is to push forward without looking back, and even if things seem impossible, remember that you serve the God of possibilities. Also, remember that He always keeps His promises. Today's text said that you will receive what He has promised if you persevere and do His will.

Despite whatever obstacle that comes your way, know that perseverance will see you through. If there is a difficulty that you are facing in your business, persevere. It really does not matter how huge that difficulty may appear in your eyes. In God's view, nothing is too big for Him to handle. Therefore, persevere. Do His will in your business and you will receive the reward that He has promised.

There may be times when it seems as though success is not in sight. Persevere, push and persist. Delays may occur so that you can get things in order. It may be that you have a lesson to learn during the waiting period. It may be that God is preparing a huge business breakthrough for you.

As your business unfolds today, please persevere and do His will. Once you do this, you will receive His promises. The good news is that God never falls short on His promises. You can count on Him to fulfill each one. God always does what He says.

~

Quiet Reflections

_____
_____
_____
_____
_____
_____
_____
_____
_____
_____

Day Seventeen

"I will instruct you and teach you in the way you should go; I will counsel you with my loving eye on you." Psalm 32:8

Some business decisions are tough. Having to answer a Board of Directors, a government agency, or your employees about a major business snafu can make you uneasy as a leader. Some entrepreneurs tell of their experience of the business keeping them up at night. This is not unreal, although the reality is that it does not have to be this way.

Whatever decisions you may have to face, God will instruct you and teach you in the way you should go. He will provide you with counsel and He will lovingly keep His eye on you and your business. When you are about to make any business decision, take it to God first so that He can instruct you and teach you.

Having God look at a situation before you make a decision will result in little to no pain or angst. If you can receive instructions and teaching from the all-wise God, there will be no need to be anxious. He has got your back. Know this without a doubt.

Seek God in a posture to receive His counsel. Sometimes He will tell you to make a decision different from what you expected or contrary to what is popular. Rest assured that

His guidance and instruction are reliable. Having someone who knows the future to rely on is a big bonus as an entrepreneur.

You may have a second in command who you rely on to run the business in your absence and you should. It is good business practice. I submit that you should have a first in command who you can always seek counsel, teaching, and instruction from to help guide you in your decision making. Since He knows the future, tapping into His power is sensible as you run your business daily. Include Him as the first stop and your decision making will be easier.

~

Quiet Reflections

_____

_____

_____

_____

_____

_____

_____

_____

_____

_____

Day Eighteen

"Let the wise listen and add to their learning, and let the discerning get guidance." Proverbs 1:5

I f you are wise in your industry that is admirable. Some entrepreneurs are ranked in the top tier within their business space. People seek your wisdom on how you do what you do. They glean inspiration from you as much as they can. They listen to your YouTube videos, subscribe to your blog, follow you on all social media platforms and they just watch your every move.

Even though you may be a high-ranking entrepreneur within your industry, the Bible states that the wise should add to their learning. There is never a point of learning that is too much and I will quickly add that no one knows everything, except God of course.

As business owners, it is important to be humble enough to keep on learning. As long as you have life, be open to learning. Be wise enough to listen and add to your learning. Additionally, the Bible encourages us to be discerning and get guidance. Some entrepreneurs are brilliant and can write about their business "with their eyes closed." Certainly, this is wisdom and can be taught to others through speaking, writing and coaching. In doing these activities of disseminating your wisdom, you can learn more and you can also practice discernment.

Using good judgment is important for entrepreneurs. God encourages us to do just that - use discernment. Being able to determine when to move forward with a client or not will require discernment. It will be required in all business decision making including whom to hire, what to invest in, which meetings to attend, pay increases, bonuses and so much more.

~

Quiet Reflections

_____

_____

_____

_____

_____

_____

_____

_____

_____

_____

Day Nineteen

"Have I not commanded you? Be strong and courageous. Do not be afraid; do not be discouraged; for the Lord, your God will be with you wherever you go." Joshua 1:9

Be strong and courageous is a command. It is a command that applies to business owners as well. To be an entrepreneur is a courageous commitment. It takes strength and mind power. Having courage is one thing, but relinquishing fear is another.

God also calls us to be fearless and to be encouraged. Being fearless does not mean being reckless. What it means is to move forward in faith. There are situations in which the feeling of abject fear may overwhelm you. Shake it off, because you have the courage and power within you to move forward without fear.

Most times the very thing that you fear is nonexistent or will not happen. Replace any fear with faith. It takes practice. Believe that you can accomplish absolutely anything with the power that God has endowed upon you. Dream big and see those dreams in your inner eyes of faith. Know that once you can think or conceive it in your mind, you can have it, it can and will happen.

Knowing this, think and conceive the items that will benefit you as an entrepreneur. In the meantime, you should not fear, but embrace faith to take the place of fear so that fear will have no place to live within your powerful vessel.

Unravel fear, weave faith and hold fast to the courage that God has called you to have. Wherever you go, remember that God will be with you. Having God with you is big. Do not be discouraged, work your faith muscles and be strong.

~

Quiet Reflections

_____
_____
_____
_____
_____
_____
_____
_____
_____
_____

Day Twenty

"Take delight in the Lord, and he will give you the desires of your heart." Psalm 37:4

Be happy in the Lord and He will give you whatever you desire, whether it is for your business or any other desire. Imagine that all God wants from you is for you to delight in Him and He will give you your heart's desire. That is one of God's prerequisites for Him to grant you what you want. To delight yourself in God is to have extreme pleasure in Him. When this happens, He will give you whatever is in the deepest recesses of your heart, the things that you yearn for deeply. The things that you, sometimes, secretly keep to yourself.

Business owners long to obtain and maintain profitability. You may have been experiencing profits for only some months here and there, but you desire to earn consistent profits. Another item of significance for business owners is having the right team to help move the business forward. Having a growing client base is always welcomed by entrepreneurs. You can have all those desires and more, because they are not far-fetched if you delight in the Lord. Once you can think of it, you can have it, and it will happen.

God is big enough to handle it all, from your personal to your business goals. He wants us to ask for big stuff because

He is a big God. The beauty of it all is that His giving is the best. His gifts are beautiful beyond measure and He is interested in giving you the desires of your heart.

~

Quiet Reflections

_____
_____
_____
_____
_____
_____
_____
_____
_____
_____

Day Twenty One

"Ask and it will be given to you; seek and you will find; knock and the door will be opened to you." Matthew 7:7

W hatever you would like for your business, all you have to do is ask and it will be given to you. It sounds simple and, in some ways, you may feel that it is impossible. You may be thinking that you have asked and have not received what you requested.

Could it be that there is a particular way to ask? Could it be that you need special words to say? Or could it be that you had to do a special ritual when you are asking? None of the above. It is asking and completely believing. Many times, we harbor a small amount of doubt not realizing it is blocking our blessings.

The Bible said it, so you can believe it. Have you ever needed something that you know that a friend of yours had and all you had to do was ask if you needed it? Did you doubt whether your friend would give it to you? Or did you ask believing that your friend would give it to you? Well, it is similar to that. The only difference is that sometimes the individual may not feel like giving it to you. With God, once He knows it is a good gift for you, He will give it, because, even though He knows all things, He would like you to ask. Asking is not difficult. It is a matter of telling God what you desire or want. He will grant it, because He is the one who is inspiring you to ask. Instead of only thinking about what you want for your business, go ahead, ask God, He will grant it. It starts with faith. It is a matter of believing without a doubt that He will fulfill your request.

God also wants you to seek, because you will find once you do that. Seek how you can continuously improve your business. While you are seeking, knock and the door of opportunities for your business will open for you. The door of abundance, good relationships and success. Ask, seek, knock and you will be rewarded with amazing gifts from the all-powerful God of the Universe.

~

Quiet Reflections

_____

_____

_____

_____

_____

_____

_____

_____

_____

_____

Day Twenty Two

"Where there is no vision, the people perish." Proverbs 29:18

Having a life vision is critical to progress and success. If you have a life vision, it follows that you will have a business vision.

If there is no vision for your business, your business will die. Think about when you leave home to head to your place of business, do you leave without any visuals of the path you will take to get there. I am positive that you have a vision of getting there. Similarly, it is essential that you see in your mind's eye where you want to go in your business. Seeing it before it happens is a vision and is more powerful than you can imagine. Therefore, I encourage you to intentionally practice seeing your desire. You can do this through the practice of meditation.

Think of where you are currently in your business. If you are totally satisfied and contented with where you are, then there is no need to read further for today. However, if there is anything that you want to improve or change, visualize it. Visualize it not only for the moment, but spend uninterrupted time, go deep in your visualization and see it happening. Don't be flippant about it, treat this activity as urgent, because it is.

See the steps that you are taking and the people who may be involved. See the date that it actually comes to pass. Then, feel the joy and other emotions you feel with having your vision come to pass.

Now that you have created your vision, replay it in your mind daily, and sometimes, more than once a day, until it comes to pass. I promise you that your vision will be realized if you are consistent and open to receiving the blessings that God has to offer as it relates to your vision.

$\sim$

Quiet Reflections

_____

_____

_____

_____

_____

_____

_____

_____

_____

_____

Day Twenty Three

"And the LORD answered me, and said, Write the vision, and make it plain upon tables, that he may run that readeth it". Habukkah 2:2

Writing down your vision is important for success. God has stated it clearly in His word. As an entrepreneur, you already know that it is critical to write your vision. But have you done so? If not, why not? Having your vision is wonderful, but taking it up a notch by writing it down is powerful.

Writing your vision works. Write what you see in your mind for you and your business. Write it down. It really does not matter if you have thought of it a million times. What matters is that you put pen to paper. Notice, I did not say to type it out. I am saying to write it down. There is power in thinking of your vision and even more power in writing it down.

The vision you write should not be limited. Remember we serve a big God. Remember too that He can do the even what seems impossible. Make your vision big. Whatever you can humanly think, you can achieve it so write it down. Take time to meditate. In your prayer, quiet, and or meditation time, God will also speak with you, giving you thoughts regarding your business. Listen out for Him. Write down whatever He tells you. There is nothing that God cannot help you to achieve as an entrepreneur. With Him, your goals are completely attainable.

If you have not written down your vision, pause, and take the time to write your vision today. Review your vision daily, ideally early in the day. This activity will prove to be rewarding.

~

Quiet Reflections

_____

_____

_____

_____

_____

_____

_____

_____

_____

Day Twenty Four

~~~~~~

"Be anxious for nothing; but in everything by
prayer and supplication with thanksgiving let your
requests be made known unto God." Philippians 4:6

As a business owner, at times anxiety sets in when
certain situations arise. I challenge you to begin your
business day with prayer and supplication. This is separate
from your prayer to start your day as a whole.

When you walk into your place of business before you
get started get into a posture of prayer. Whatever posture
you feel comfortable taking on. God is more concerned
about an earnest heart rather than whether you are kneeling,
standing, or sitting. If you do not have a bricks, mortar business, or you work remotely, before you begin any business
dealings for the day, you too should get into a posture of
prayer. Not only do I recommend prayer before you start
your business day, but at the end as well. As a matter of fact,
during the day if you begin to get anxious, jump into prayer.

Use whatever prayer posture that you and God determine, whether it is standing, sitting, laying, kneeling, walking, or a mixture. The most important thing is to get into a
prayer posture. Prayer is not necessarily thou and thine and
other popular cliches. It is genuinely telling God exactly
what is on your heart, your gratitude, your fears, your joys,
for your employees, your clients, your stakeholders, your

requests for guidance, or to solve a problem, how much you are in awe of His works and whatever else is on your heart. Don't get bogged down in how long your prayer is - it can be as short or as long as you need - the important thing is the genuineness with which you communicate with God almighty. After all, He knows our hearts.

Praying only when you are anxious or in need is not ideal, but at the beginning and end of your business day at least.

~

Quiet Reflections

_____

_____

_____

_____

_____

_____

_____

_____

_____

_____

Day Twenty Five

"For God hath not given us the spirit of fear; but of power, and of love, and of a sound mind". 2 Timothy 1:7

Certainly, sometimes fear creeps in when things are not going as planned in your business, but God has not given you the spirit of fear. When you are fearful in your business, know that it is not from God.

God has given you the spirit of "power, love and a sound mind." When fear tries to find its way in your heart, as it relates to your business or any other matter, reject it boldly. Know that you have the power to overcome fear and solve any problems you may face. Power from God is huge and can equip you to overcome obstacles that may seem too big to handle. The magnitude really does not matter. It can be problems regarding financials, taxes, hiring, firing, clients, budget, whatever it is, you can overcome with the spirit of faith that is so freely given to you by God Almighty.

There is more good news - God has also given you the spirit of love. Perfect love creates an environment where fear cannot live. Self-love is very important and so is love for others. Exercising love as an entrepreneur will give you confidence that you can use to guide how you treat others and how you treat yourself. Loving yourself also includes protecting your mind.

God is so very wonderful to you that He has given you a sound mind, a sharp mind. A mind that you can use to discern and grow. A mind that will not do well with entertaining fear. A mind that will flourish in faith.

Embrace the spirit of power, love and a sound mind to run your business each day.

~

Quiet Reflections

_____

_____

_____

_____

_____

_____

_____

_____

_____

_____

Day Twenty Six

"For as he thinketh in his heart, so is he." Proverbs 23:7

Dealing with a multitude of situations is unavoidable as an entrepreneur. Your character tells who you are in business and guides decision-making. Everything that you do stems from your mind whether it is positive or negative. This is where our verse for today becomes real.

The actions you take daily tell others how you think. There is no way that you can be thinking one way but acting another. And, if that becomes the case, eventually, the truth will come out. Doing the right thing is sometimes difficult for entrepreneurs, especially when money is involved. Sometimes entrepreneurs get involved in dishonest business dealings. For instance, they may take actions to keep another business leader down so that their business can succeed. Sometimes underhanded actions are unfortunately taken. These actions are watered in the mind before being expressed externally. As an entrepreneur, you will do well to check the actions of your business colleagues, employees, and others. Actions will speak volumes given that "as a man (woman) thinketh so is he (she)."

It is rare that a person's action does not match who he is in truth and in fact. It was Maya Angelo who said, "when

people show you who they are, believe them the first time."
When anyone has shown actions that you question, go
ahead, and believe that this is who they are as a person.
Certainly, people can change but you would know when
people have changed because their actions will match. If you
lock hands with God, and walk with Him daily, He will
endow you with a healthy dose of discernment. You will
know when actions match the person and who you can
trust.

When weighing your decisions regarding business
matters, remember that "as a man thinketh, so is he."

~

Quiet Reflections

_____
_____
_____
_____
_____
_____
_____
_____
_____
_____

Day Twenty Seven

"But seek ye first the kingdom of God, and his righteousness; and all these things shall be added unto you." Matthew 6:33

E ntrepreneurs have goals and aspirations for their businesses. Certainly, asking God to help you with these is one of the very important steps you can take. Another critical step which should be the first step is putting God's Kingdom first. Yet another key action is doing what is right.

Putting God's Kingdom first as an entrepreneur is prioritizing the things of God and letting the rest fall in place. Seeking means searching like you have lost something very important. When a person loses something that is important to them, they do all they can to find it. They ask people for help, they do research, they do their very best to figure out how to find it, even if it takes a long time. This is the attitude that God wants you to have as an entrepreneur when you are seeking His Kingdom.

In addition to seeking God's Kingdom, you are encouraged to also seek His righteousness. His righteousness involves taking actions that will promote the Kingdom of God. At the point at which God sees you seeking His Kingdom and His righteousness, He will fulfill His promise by fulfilling your needs including that of your business. On top of all that, He will add your desires for your business to the equation. He will cause your business to flourish, and He will give you the wisdom necessary to take your business to higher levels.

Genuinely seeking the Kingdom of God and His righteousness is packed with several rewards for you and your business.

~

Quiet Reflections

_____

_____

_____

_____

_____

_____

_____

_____

_____

_____

Day Twenty Eight

"Whoever can be trusted with very little can also be trusted with much." Luke 16:10

Whatever you have now as an entrepreneur, ensure that God can trust you with it. If He can trust you with what you have now, He will add to it and He will trust you with more.

If per chance you don't have all that you need in your business, allow God to trust you and He will provide more. Most entrepreneurs want to have abundance and overflow – more clients, more customers, more profits, more money, more donations, more deals, more real estate, more, more and more. It is great to want more though some think that God wants them to have just enough or not enough. God is a God of overflow, and He wants us to thrive in our businesses. There should be no doubt, because that is His desire for us. The overarching question is, can God trust you with what He has already given to you?

God has made ways for you at various points. He has given you tangible and intangible blessings. Do you consistently offer up gratitude to Him for your blessings? Do you use your blessings to bless others? Are you showing appreciation by growing what He has already given you? These are some of the questions that you should be asking yourself as a business leader.

Taking an introspective perspective when it comes to figuring out if you are appreciative for your current blessings is a method that can yield great rewards.

In this reflective approach, asking yourself these pointed questions will get you to think and will even influence you to adopt a grateful and appreciative spirit. In turn, God will reward your gratitude with bestowing more upon you. Your appreciation will also be rewarded. Being appreciative involves acknowledging what you already have and caring for it.

The crux of the matter is that God will reward you and trust you with more if you show him that you are a good steward of what you have now.

~

Quiet Reflections

_____

_____

_____

_____

_____

_____

_____

_____

_____

Day Twenty Nine

"Ye have not, because ye ask not." James 4:2

There are times when our business may be in lack. It does not have to be that way. The word of God says in essence that if we ask, we will receive. If this is one of God's promises, then why do some business owners not implement it?

If a good friend of yours has something you need, you will most likely ask, because you know you will get it. It is with this confidence that you ask for what you want for your business. God cares about the success of your business, and He is ready to give you your desires.

It really does not matter how big your request is for your business. It really does not matter how impossible it appears to you. He is the God of the impossibilities and He can deliver without a doubt. For the men, think back to high school when there was this one girl who was drop-dead gorgeous and you wished that you could go out with her, but you were too scared to ask. You talked with your friends about her and they encouraged you to ask her out. You mustered up the courage, asked her out and she said yes without effort. In this example, you did not keep talking about it, but you moved into action and asked, receiving the results you desired.

While this example was a very different situation, the concept is the same, "you have not, because you ask not." Whatever you desire, you can ask God for it. Asking includes believing. It is important that you stay away from asking amiss.

Ask in faith and without doubt. Ask and you will receive what you desire for your business.

～

Quiet Reflections

_____
_____
_____
_____
_____
_____
_____
_____
_____
_____

Day Thirty

"In the morning, LORD, you hear my voice;
in the morning I lay my requests before you
and wait expectantly." Psalm 5:3

When you develop and implement a marketing campaign for your business, you expect to see clients, customers, sales, and visibility on the rise. You expect to see positive business results. Once you see these results, you know that your campaign worked, and you are inclined to repeat the steps that brought you success. It is this kind of expectancy that must be practiced after you make your requests to God.

Let the Lord hear you in the morning, make your requests to him and wait in anticipation for the results you desire. There is something about going before God in the morning. Your mind is fresh and is not influenced by concerns. It is rich, ready for meditation and being one with God. Use the morning to give your fresh and first praises of the day to God and make your requests to Him. Be earnest and let you conversation with God flow as it would with a good friend whom you are excited to talk things over with at that point.

There is no need to use fancy or impressive words. It is not an interview. Rather it is the development of a deeper connection with the God of this Universe. While it is unnecessary to figure out how to impress God, it is very necessary to speak from the heart. He values heart conversations. Once you make your requests to God in the morning, expect Him to move in a way that can blow your mind.

Waiting expectantly and being in tune with Him makes a world of a difference for you and your business.

∽

Quiet Reflections

_____

_____

_____

_____

_____

_____

_____

_____

_____

_____

Day Thirty One

"If you remain in me and my words remain in you, ask whatever you wish, and it will be done for you." John 15:7

Sometimes people see God as someone who is there to solve problems and give us what we need. As a result, folks tend to run to him when they need something or when a major issue is going on that needs divine intervention. There is nothing wrong with running to God to ask for things, or to ask him to solve an issue for you. There should be more to it than that, though.

Reading God's word daily, letting it take lodgment in your heart and remaining grounded in Him is what entrepreneurs should strive for constantly. When God's word is within you, it is shown through your actions, the words you speak and how you deal with and treat others. When you allow God's word to guide your speech and actions, then you can ask Him for ANYTHING and it will be done for you.

Entrepreneurs have the amazing opportunity to ask for anything and get a favorable response. Knowing this should motivate you to read God's word and develop that intimate relationship with Him that can withstand any business challenges that may arise.

Yes, it is acceptable to ask God for things and ask Him to

do things for your business. It is also acceptable to ask Him to solve issues that you may face as an entrepreneur. It is not acceptable to do all this in a vacuum. Rather, take in His word and remain in Him, and let His words remain in you. The rest will fall perfectly into place.

~

Quiet Reflections

_____

_____

_____

_____

_____

_____

_____

_____

_____

_____

Day Thirty Two

"The LORD himself goes before you and will be with you; he will never leave you nor forsake you." Deuteronomy 31:8

I f you must run a marathon, it is a good idea to visit the path ahead of time to see what it is like and to get an idea of how you will proceed. It builds your motivation and mental readiness. Some runners sit and visualize themselves making it to the finish line, but what if you had someone go ahead of you to review the path for you? Then, they report to you in crisp detail how the path is and recommend how you can make it to the finish line.

My friend, in this business marathon, God goes before you, and He also goes with you. He scopes out everything, He makes recommendations, and the beauty of it all, is that He stays with you - He never leaves you.

Many entrepreneurs wish that they had someone to guide them on their decisions or tell them exactly what they should do to increase sales or profits. There is someone who already knows in depth how it all works. That someone has already seen ahead. He has the best recommendations and guidance necessary for your business success. He is willing to stay by your side for the entire journey without missing a beat.

Allow the God who has gone before you and who

knows your business inside out to walk with you. Allow Him to give you all the tools necessary to run your business successfully. It does not necessarily happen overnight, but rather a daily walk and a close connection will allow you to reap the benefits that are freely offered to you as a business owner.

~

Quiet Reflections

_____

_____

_____

_____

_____

_____

_____

_____

_____

_____

Day Thirty Three

"For the love of money is a root of all kinds
of evil." 1 Timothy 6:10

The "Love of Money," as used in the Bible, has been a very controversial and misunderstood topic. Be realistic, if you don't love money enough to work for it, then how will you live? Everything costs money whether it is your home (rent or own), utilities, gas for your car, cable, groceries, phone, and everything that allows you to survive on earth. You simply cannot live comfortably without money. The reality is that money comes in to play for all of it.

If a business owner is stating that he does not love money, then money will not be attracted to that business. The misunderstanding comes about, because of those who love money to the extent that they allow it to guide their every action which can lead to evil results. Loving money is one thing, because it serves us: acceptable. Loving money when you have placed it first in life is another thing: unacceptable. Guidance on the topic of loving money is in the word of God.

In Ecclesiastes the Bible states that "money answers all things." It means that wealth can meet the needs of food, shelter, clothing and the like. It is not a statement to mean that money should take first place over God or people. The lack of money can be very distressing and can lead to poor choices. Looking at why some people rob banks or get involved in fraudulent activities reveals that most times it is because they lack money. These are examples of how poor choices can be made when money is lacking.

Money is very important and answers all things, but it should not take the place of love for God and humanity. To get over the apparent confusion when it comes to loving money, stay in tune with God and His will for your life and business. Go ahead; it is acceptable to love money.

~

Quiet Reflections

_____

_____

_____

_____

_____

_____

_____

_____

_____

_____

Day Thirty Four

"He held fast to the Lord and did not stop
following him; he kept the commands the
Lord had given Moses. And the Lord was with
him; he was successful in whatever he
undertook." 2 Kings 18:6-7

When the going gets tough, some tend to leave God's side thinking that He does not care anymore. It is at that time that it is necessary to hold fast to God and keep following Him. If you want to be successful in whatever you take on, follow God's commandments and remain committed to following Him daily.

Remain steadfast in following God and you will experience the success you desire in your business. Following God is not meant to be fanatical. It is about allowing His word to guide you and your business. It is about treating others fairly and it is about doing the right thing even when no one is looking.

As a business owner, your customers, clients, employees, board, competitors, and other stakeholders are all people you may be interacting with at one point or another. It can sometimes take a lot from a business leader to remain circumspect in all business dealings. The good news is that it is indeed possible.

There is a world of possibilities when you follow God and keep His commands. One of the greatest possibilities is that whatever you undertake, you will be successful.

Knowing this should boost your business confidence and inspire you to stay aligned with God.

~

Quiet Reflections

_____

_____

_____

_____

_____

_____

_____

_____

_____

_____

Day Thirty Five

~~~

"But as for you, be strong and do not give up, for your work will be rewarded." 2 Chronicles 15:7

Be strong is a phrase that people spit out when something that weighs heavily on your emotions has occurred. It is easy to say the phrase, but can you easily grasp the phrase and activate it during a tough time? I am sure you can.

Tough situations may arise and you would have to pull on those two words: *be strong*. Thankfully, it does not end there. The next part of this verse says: *and do not give up*. Remaining firm and intentionally not giving up has its rewards. Many times, just when you feel like the only thing left to do is give up, your work will be rewarded. This is one reason to keep pushing forward. Your breakthrough blessing can come when you are at the brink of giving up.

Giving up should not be an option. God has placed the business idea in your mind for a reason. Allow Him to fulfill that reason by surrendering your business to Him. Let Him serve as your Chief Executive Officer and as the Chair of your Board of Directors. Each decision you make as the head of your business should go through God and should be sanctioned by Him. It will not happen overnight. It takes having that daily walk and daily talk with God. It takes practice to lean on Him for everything. Eventually, it will come naturally and all the work that you have been doing will indeed be rewarded.

Rewards can come in the form of additional contracts, grants, customers, revenue, recognition and more. Thankfully, you can be assured that if you remain consistent and never give up, you will see the fruits of your work.

~

Quiet Reflections

_____

_____

_____

_____

_____

_____

_____

_____

_____

_____

Day Thirty Six

"Oh, that you would bless me and enlarge my territory! Let your hand be with me and keep me from harm so that I will be free from pain." And God granted his request." 1 Chronicles 4:10

Many times, during prayer, people ask God to bless them or their family members or even their plans. This means that people believe that blessings are good and positive. Blessings are indeed beautiful. Taking the "bless me" prayer up a notch by adding the word, indeed. Indeed, is a means to emphasize the preceding point. Bless me indeed is a request for definite blessings.

As a business owner you can ask God to bless your business indeed. He will provide supernatural blessings. Blessings that you have not even thought of will come upon you and your business. This prayer goes further and it says "...and enlarge my territory." A territory is a big area, it can cover a street, a city, a county, a state, a country, or countries. Asking God to enlarge your business territory is a loaded prayer. God will bless your business indeed and enlarge your business territory. Enlarging your territory does not necessarily have to do with geography. It can be geared towards expansion and enlargement in customers or clients, profits, relationships and more.

Asking God to bless and enlarge your territory is important. It is even more important that you firmly believe that

He will answer that request. Speaking it, seeing it and believing it will result in bringing it to fruition.

Let your prayer today be "bless my business indeed and enlarge my territory." Such a prayer can result in stretching and expansion that you may not realize could occur within yourself and your business.

The possibilities are endless when God enlarges your territory and blesses you indeed.

~

Quiet Reflections

_____

_____

_____

_____

_____

_____

_____

_____

_____

_____

Day Thirty Seven

"Seek the Lord and his strength, seek his
face continually." 1 Chronicles 16:11

Look for God and look for His strength without
stopping. This should be a daily practice. To seek is to
look for something intently with effort.

When you misplace your keys, particularly when you are
about to head to an important meeting, you put energy,
focus, intention and effort into finding that key. Similarly,
these are the types of force that you as a business owner
should embrace when seeking the Lord and His strength.
His strength is made perfect in weakness.

In any moments that you may feel weak, He is available
to give you the strength that you need. However, this
strength is given when you seek it out fervently. How you go
about seeking God is important. Staying connected with
Him requires intention and consistent prayer, meditation
and devotion. During these practices, it is important to
listen to what God is telling you. He speaks to us moment
by moment. There are times that we are distracted by the
daily cares that we do not hear His voice clearly. Be intentional about listening to hear what God has to say to you
daily. You will be amazed by the details with which he
communicates with you.

You will be excited to move forward on your journey as an entrepreneur as you seek God's face continually for you and your business.

~

Quiet Reflections

_____

_____

_____

_____

_____

_____

_____

_____

_____

_____

Day Thirty Eight

⚬⚬⚬

"And I have filled him with the spirit of God, in wisdom, and in understanding, and in knowledge, and in all manner of workmanship..." Exodus 31:33

God has granted you wisdom, understanding, knowledge and workmanship. How cool is that? Someone who is all-knowing has given you these tools. Accept them and use them in your business and your life.

Embrace these divine gifts that God has offered to you and spread your wings to soar like an eagle in your field of business. Not only are these gifts divine, but they are also free. It is a matter of opening your heart to accept them.

As business owners, it is sometimes difficult to move away from your normal way of operating. Understanding that for success to occur, you would need to operate differently is a key step. Taking the same actions month after month without the kind of results you desire simply means that your actions need to change. It has been said that "insanity is doing the same thing over and over while expecting different results." Certainly, you don't want to feel like you are insane, consequently you are encouraged to stay away from those behaviors.

Be intentional about your actions and note what works and what does not. There is no need to keep doing the things in your business that do not work. God has created us with a powerfully creative mind. Sit in His presence and let Him give you what He said He will: wisdom, understanding, knowledge and workmanship. These skills will no doubt help your business tremendously.

~

Quiet Reflections

_____
_____
_____
_____
_____
_____
_____
_____
_____
_____

Day Thirty Nine

"Honor the LORD with your wealth, with the
first fruits of all your crops..." Proverbs 3:9

Honor is important. If you have ever been honored,
you know that you are treated as royalty and you are
set apart from others. Honoring God "with your wealth and
with your first fruits of ALL your crops" is rewarding.
Ensuring that your wealth is used in such a way to bring
honor to God is an entrepreneurial success secret.

It is not complicated. It is very straightforward. Honor
God with your wealth. Let Him be the first to be honored
when you earn money or any increase. You can honor God
by returning to Him a faithful tithe, giving back to the poor
and needy, designating funds to ministries that serve the
community and looking for ways to bless others with your
wealth.

An entrepreneur may argue that they are not wealthy if
the business is not performing at the height that is expected.
If you have determined that you are not gaining sufficient
revenue, then you have an opportunity to do so by applying
the principles established within this forty-day journey.

Walking in step with God, allowing Him to transform
you as a business leader, can take you and your business to
the next level and to heights that you had not imagined.

Open your heart and mind to where God wants to take you and your business and embrace the journey.

Honoring God with your first fruits as a business owner gives an excellent platform for growing your business wealth.

~

Quiet Reflections

_____

_____

_____

_____

_____

_____

_____

_____

_____

_____

Day Forty

"Finally, my brethren, be strong in the Lord,
and in the power of his might." Ephesians 6:10

Be strong is what many tell you when you are going through a rough patch. Merely saying it seems to feel good for the person who is giving that encouragement, but what does it really mean when you are told to be strong?

Being strong can take on various meanings depending on your perspective. One thing is clear and that is it is not referring to physical strength. Allow me to take a different outlook. Being strong means you do not necessarily have all the answers. It means that you can reach for strength from a higher source - God. It means that you can act in faith, that you can "call those things that are not as though they were..." It means that there is light at the end of any darkness that you may experience. It means that you have brighter days to look forward to seeing.

Be strong in the power of God's might means that you can count on His power to help you. "Your strength is made perfect in weakness." If ever you feel that you need added strength to run your business, remember that God has got your back and He has strength that you can tap into.

As an entrepreneur, you may have ups and downs that may come your way. Just remember to "be strong" and keep going! Remember that you are an eagle in every sense of the word and an eagle has undeniable strength.

∼

Quiet Reflections

_____
_____
_____
_____
_____
_____
_____
_____
_____
_____

Commitment

I, [insert your name], commit myself and my business to God. I believe that He loves me and wants me to succeed like an eagle. I am confident that He desires the best for me and my business. Throughout this forty-day journey, I have been reminded and I am convinced that God created me with a powerful mind that can achieve anything I set my mind to.

The following are my commitments:

1. I commit to daily prayer, devotion and meditation.
2. I commit to expressing gratitude every day.
3. I commit to acknowledging the power within me created by God.
4. I commit to consistently seeking the face of God for guidance in my life and business.
5. I commit to allowing God to guide my decision-making.
6. I commit to running my business with guidance from God.
7. I commit to listening to God for what He says directly to me.
8. I commit to caring for my mind, body, and soul so that I can be the best version of myself as I walk the earth.
9. I commit to writing down my vision.
10. I commit to treating my employees, clients, customers, and stakeholders with the same love and care that God has for me.
11. I commit to rewarding others when necessary.

12. I commit to practicing integrity within my business.
13. I commit to giving myself grace, knowing that God has already given me grace.
14. I commit to getting back up if I fall.
15. I commit to having the faith that God will exceed my business expectations.
16. I commit to loving myself enough to stay committed and consistent.
17. I commit to accepting all of God's gifts for me.
18. I commit to working diligently in my business.
19. I commit to becoming a successful entrepreneur without a doubt.
20. I commit to loving God enough to trust Him completely.

Made in the USA
Middletown, DE
10 December 2023

44198128R00053